I'M (CAN WE STILL BE FRIENDS) SORRY

summersdale

I'M SORRY (CAN WE STILL BE FRIENDS?)

Summersdale Publishers Ltd
46 West Street
Chichester
West Sussex
PO19 1RP
UK

www.summersdale.com

Printed and bound in China

ISBN: 978-1-84953-376-8

Substantial discounts on bulk quantities of Summersdale books are available to corporations, professional associations and other organisations. For details contact Nicky Douglas by telephone: +44 (0) 1243 756902, fax +44 (0) 1243 786300 or email: nicky@summersdale.com.

TO..............................

FROM.......................

WE'VE HAD THE BREAK-UP

CAN WE HAVE THE
MAKE-UP?

THE WEATHER SEEMS BETTER WHEN WE'RE FRIENDS

HERE ARE MY *BEST* PUPPY DOG EYES

**BE TRUE TO
YOUR WORK
YOUR WORD
AND
YOUR FRIEND**

HENRY DAVID THOREAU

LIFE IS AN

IN

NORMAN COUSINS

"

I HAVE FRIENDS IN
OVERALLS
WHOSE FRIENDSHIP
I WOULD NOT SWAP
FOR THE FAVOUR
OF THE **KINGS**
OF THE **WORLD**

THOMAS EDISON

I'M STOPPING BEING

DASTARDLY

AND STARTING BEING
DELIGHTFUL

I'VE BEEN SHABBY...

...CAN WE PATCH THINGS UP?

FUN
ISN'T AS FUN
WITHOUT YOU

SORRY INFINITY

TO **ERR** IS HUMAN
TO **FORGIVE** DIVINE

ALEXANDER POPE

FRIENDSHIP IS A SINGLE SOUL DWELLING IN TWO BODIES

ARISTOTLE

YOU'RE A FIRST-CLASS FRIEND
BUT I'VE BEEN AN

WHEN YOU *FORGIVE* YOU IN NO WAY CHANGE THE PAST — *BUT YOU SURE DO* CHANGE THE FUTURE

BERNARD MELTZER

YOU WILL **ALWAYS** HAVE MY FRIENDSHIP

(AND THAT **BOOK YOU BORROWED**)

I'VE BEEN THE VILLAIN OF THE PIECE

MY BEST

FRIEND

IS THE ONE WHO

BRINGS OUT THE *BEST* IN ME

—————————

HENRY FORD

I'VE BEEN
A *RIGHT*
NOGGIN

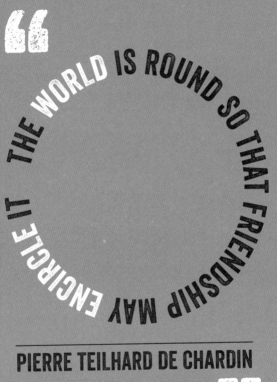

"THE WORLD IS ROUND SO THAT FRIENDSHIP MAY ENCIRCLE IT

PIERRE TEILHARD DE CHARDIN

ES TUT MIR LEID

JE SUIS DÉSOLÉE

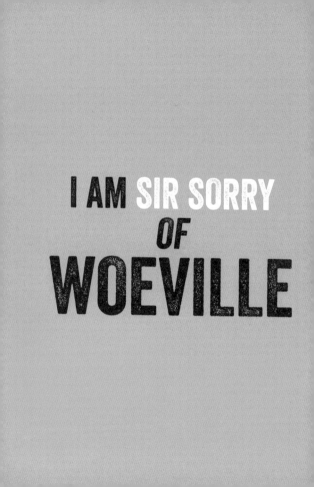

SOME PEOPLE GO TO PRIESTS
OTHERS TO POETRY
I TO MY FRIENDS

VIRGINIA WOOLF

(NB AM WILLING
TO AIR-KISS,
PECK, SMOOCH
OR NOSE RUB)

HOW
CAN I MAKE IT UP
TO YOU?

"

FORGIVENESS
IS A GIFT
YOU GIVE
YOURSELF

SUZANNE SOMERS

"

FRIENDSHIP
MULTIPLIES
THE GOOD OF LIFE
AND DIVIDES
THE EVIL

BALTASAR GRACIAN

LET ME BUY YOU DINNER

IT
WILL BE
A TASTY
MOUNTAIN OF SCRUMPTIOUS

I'M ALL
THE *SORRIES*
OF THE
RAINBOW

I'VE BEEN PANTS

(BIG GREY GRUBBY ONES)

I'VE PUT MYSELF ON THE NAUGHTY STEP

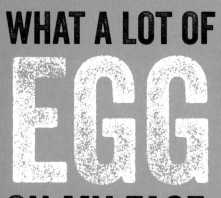

WHAT A LOT OF
EGG
ON MY FACE

(HAVE AN OMELETTE
WITH ME?)

"

FORGIVENESS SAVES THE EXPENSE OF ANGER THE COST OF HATRED THE WASTE OF SPIRITS

HANNAH MORE

"

PLEASE ADD A
SPOONFUL OF SORRY
TO MY
HUMBLE PIE

THE MOST I CAN DO FOR MY FRIEND IS SIMPLY BE HIS FRIEND

HENRY DAVID THOREAU

WILL YOU ACCEPT MY FRIENDSHIP REQUEST?

**IT TAKES ONE PERSON
TO FORGIVE
IT TAKES TWO PEOPLE
TO BE REUNITED**

LEWIS B. SMEDES

LET'S PUT THE

BAD TIMES
BEHIND US

AND THE
GOOD TIMES
IN FRONT

(I'M TRULY SORRY I WAS ROTTEN TO *YOU*)

I SEND YOU
ALL MY SORRIES
(WRAPPED IN ALL MY SADS)

CAN WE
WIPE THE
SLATE
CLEAN?

LET'S *TURN* OVER

A NEW LEAF

TOGETHER

(THE LEAF IS QUITE HEAVY

IT HAS TO BE TOGETHER)

FORGIVENESS
IS A *FUNNY THING*

IT WARMS THE HEART

AND COOLS
THE STING

WILLIAM ARTHUR WARD

A FRIEND IS ONE WHO KNOWS YOU AND LOVES YOU JUST THE SAME

ELBERT HUBBARD

TODAY
I'M *WEARING* MY
SORRY SOCKS
AND MY
APOLOGY PANTS

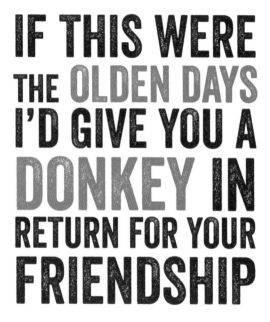

WILL YOU COME
AND BE
CAPTAIN
OF MY
FRIENDSHIP
TEAM?

I'M SORRY FROM THE
TIPS OF MY TOES

TO THE
TOP OF MY NOSE

"

A QUARREL BETWEEN FRIENDS
WHEN MADE UP ADDS A
NEW TIE TO
FRIENDSHIP

ST FRANCIS DE SALES

"

IOU
ONE GREAT BIG HUG

I'VE BEEN A BIT RUBBISH BUT I WANT TO CLEAR THINGS UP

YOU DESERVE ONLY TIP-TOP TREATMENT

I
HUMBLY BEG
YOUR APOLOGIES

FORGIVENESS
IS THE HIGHEST
VIRTUE

THE MAHABHARATA

"ALL YOU NEED TO DO TO BE MY FRIEND IS LIKE ME

TAYLOR SWIFT

"

QUITE SIMPLY
AND WITH
NO FURTHER ADO
I'M SORRY

I HAD YOUR
FRIENDSHIP VALUED

AND IT WAS
PRICELESS

WHAT A
SORRY SAUSAGE
I AM

"

THE **GREATEST GIFT**
OF LIFE
IS *FRIENDSHIP*
AND I HAVE
RECEIVED IT

HUBERT H. HUMPHREY

"

I REALLY
TRULY
AM TERRIBLY
SORRY

YOUR FRIENDSHIP
IS THE
EIGHTH WONDER
OF THE
WORLD

IF YOU'RE INTERESTED IN FINDING OUT MORE ABOUT OUR
GIFT BOOKS, FOLLOW US ON TWITTER:
@SUMMERSDALE

WWW.SUMMERSDALE.COM